THE GOLDEN YEARS

1959

text: David Sandison

design: Paul Kurzeja

SIENA

The last year of a decade is often spent in an orgy of reflection about the events which have helped shape the past ten years. It's so much easier to do than face the prospect of future uncertainties, that's for certain.

If the 1950s can be summed up simply, it's probably fair to say that they were the time when the world's youth first ceased being miniature versions of their parents and found their own voice, their own music, their own fashions and began to use them all to create their own waves. Those waves would, of course, crash on to the shores of the 1960s and make even bigger waves of their own.

For now, however, young people were content simply to have rock 'n' roll, a pantheon of heroes who owed nothing to the older generation, and a growing awareness that they could maybe make the future better than the past.

That past included the horrors of the Korean War, the bloody turmoil which marked so many countries' attempts to gain independence from colonial rule, the awful and brutal tragedy which had been the Hungarian Revolution, white and black meeting on the civil rights battlefields of the American South, and the senseless fiasco of Suez, when British and French forces tried, and failed, to inflict the old order's will on the new Arab world of

Egypt's Gamal Nasser.

Over it all, and through it all, loomed the shadow of the grown-ups' most terrifying toy - The Bomb.

There were good things too, though. Mankind began to reach towards the stars. Science found a cure for polio, the dreaded killer of children. Great art was created. The last piles of rubble left from World War II began to vanish forever, replaced by new homes, new places of work and - occasionally - astounding examples of modern architecture.

The 1950s - and 1959 in particular - offered a mass of contradictions. To misquote Charles Dickens, it was often the worst of times...but it was also the best of times.

3

Castro Victorious As Batistá Flees Havana

FIDEL CASTRO (pictured with Manuel Urrutia), the Cuban rebel guerrilla leader once dismissed as no more than a romantic no-hoper, today emerged as victor in his two-year battle to overthrow the corrupt Mafia-backed regime of President Fulgencio Batistá, who announced his intention to quit Havana at a New Year's Eve party. Dr Manuel Urrutia has been named as Batistá's successor, but observers believe his period in office will only last until Castro chooses to assume power.

For the time being the 32 year old revolutionary, who has denied he is a communist, is busy leading his forces in mopping up the last vestiges of army resistance. This has been minimal. This afternoon, when Castro's troops reached Camp Columbia, the Havana military stronghold and HQ, they entered unopposed. Groups of lightly-armed Castro supporters have been able to commandeer most of Havana's main hotels, turning them into dormitory hostels for those who will follow.

Only two nights ago those same hotels were the setting for the kind of over-the-top wining and dining, gambling and widespread prostitution for which Cuba had become infamous during Batistá's seven-year reign, when American crime syndicates used the island as a paradise resort and tax haven.

It appears that Batistá told Cuban Senate leaders he was leaving for the Dominican Republic at one such party at Camp Columbia. After toasting Cuba with champagne, he announced his departure, blaming Castro's superior armament for his defeat.

He could have added 'popular support' to his excuse. When Batistá's departure was confirmed on Havana radio, thousands of people flooded on to the capital's streets to celebrate, trashing a government newspaper office, setting a casino alight and looting stores.

Although the United States maintained a cautious silence on Castro's success, the British government would recognise his government five days later - a little over two years after he had returned to Cuba from enforced exile in Mexico, where he was trained in the guerrilla warfare techniques which have served him so well.

Cooper Beats London

Henry Cooper became the new British and Empire heavyweight champion tonight when he won a gruelling 15-round battle with Brian London, the Blackpool-born title holder, to complete a run of three comeback wins after his disastrous 1957 defeats by Swedish champion Ingemar Johansson and fellow Brit Joe Erskine. Overcoming a badly cut eye - an injury to which the South London-based fighter seems prone - Cooper gained the title he first tried to wrest from Joe Bygraves in 1957 when he lasted only nine rounds. Cooper's 1958 wins were against Dick Richardson and American Zora Folley, and tonight's victory at Earl's Court confirms the early promise of a boxer who once held the ABA's light-heavyweight title and represented Britain at the Helsinki Olympic Games in 1952.

JANUARY 27

Russia Claims Space Race Lead With Lunik

Soviet leader Nikita Khrushchev today claimed that the USSR has a clear space race lead over the United States following the successful launch of *Lunik*, the first spacecraft to escape the earth's gravity and travel into deep space.

Lunik was launched from the Soviet space centre early this month, on a trajectory intended to take it past the moon and into an orbit round the sun. While the US Space Agency responded on January 12 with an announcement confirming it had placed a contract for a capsule capable of carrying a man into orbit, experts believe that the USSR's plans for manned space flight are also well advanced, with Lunik's launch proof of a Soviet lead in rocket technology.

The US has consistently trailed Russia since October 1957, when *Sputnik-1* became the first man-made satellite to orbit the earth. That success was followed a month later when the Soviets put *Laika*, a small cross-bred husky, into space. Early US launches have been dogged by failure, with a number of rockets destroyed on the launch pad.

World Champ Hawthorn Killed In Sports Car Crash

JANUARY 22

Mike Hawthorn, the 29 year old reigning world motor racing champion, was killed today when his sports car crashed on the Guildford by-pass (pictured), close to his Surrey home. He had only recently announced his decision to retire from the sport while at the top.

A handsome, dashing figure, Hawthorn signalled his appearance on the scene in 1952 when he won two races against leading world drivers on the Goodwood circuit.

Signed to drive for Jaguar, he was soon a top-ranked racer and won the 1955 Le Mans 24-hour race - an event controversially allowed to continue after the horrific death of 85 spectators when a Mercedes ploughed into a track-side stand. Driving for Ferrari during most of his Grand Prix career, Hawthorn became world champion last October, beating his long-time friend and rival Stirling Moss by a single point.

End Credits For Movie Showman De Mille

CECIL B DE MILLE, one of the pioneers who transformed the tiny California township of Hollywood into the film capital of the world and came to personify the breed of autocratic producer-directors with his vast Biblical epics, died today in the city he helped create. He was 77.

Sent to California by the equally-autocratic Sam Goldwyn in 1913, de Mille rented a barn for $75 a month as his production base for *The Squaw Man,* the first full-length Western. A number of other pioneer film-makers had already set up shop in the Los Angeles suburb and Goldwyn took de Mille's advice to do likewise.

Producer and/or director of sex comedies in the 1920s, of adventure movies in the next two decades, and of huge-scale big-budget epics like *Samson and Delilah, The Ten Commandments* and the Barnum bio-pic *The Greatest Show On Earth* in the last few years of his life, de Mille actually made three versions of *The Squaw Man,* in 1913, 1918 and 1931, and two of *The Ten Commandments,* in 1923 and 1956.

De Mille's last great triumphs came in the 1952 Academy Awards when he stepped up, as producer, to take the Best Picture Oscar for *The Greatest Show On Earth,* and had the disappointment of losing the Director prize to John Ford softened by winning the annual Thalberg Award, reserved as the Academy's tribute for long-time distinction in the production field.

Windscale-Leukemia Links To Be Investigated

Confronted by a mounting campaign claiming links between the 1957 fire at the Windscale atomic plant in Cumberland and a recent increase in reported cases of leukemia in the area, the British government today announced the formation of a committee to investigate the claims.

In October 1957 one of the Windscale piles was permanently shut down when fire broke out and what was called 'substantial' amounts of radioactive material escaped up the plutonium manufacturing plant's 500-foot chimney. The official line was that most of the radioactivity was carried out to sea by the wind and there was no direct hazard to the public.

Thousands of gallons of locally-produced milk were poured down drains (and into the Irish Sea) as a precautionary measure, but successive health ministers and Atomic Energy Authority spokesmen have denied any possible link between those events and local doctors' concern at rising incidents of leukemia.

Britain Switches To Television

While the world's leading film-makers try to dam the flow away from cinemas, a BBC report today confirmed their worst fears: the number of TV sets now in British homes continues to climb, and the hours spent watching the box every week are also on the increase.

The report indicates that two-thirds of Britain's 37.8 million population now own a TV - an increase of almost five million in the past two years. And those with sets are now watching for more than 12 hours a week - an hour more than in 1957.

Plane Crash Claims Rock Stars Holly, Valens And Bopper

THE POP MUSIC WORLD WAS in mourning today as it learned of the death in a plane crash of Buddy Holly, Ritchie Valens and JP Richardson, better known as The Big Bopper. The three entertainers and the pilot of the small plane they'd hired to fly them to the next stage of a mid-West tour, were all killed outright when the aircraft crashed in a snowstorm (pictured) shortly after leaving Mason City, Iowa.

Holly's death robbed popular music of one of its most talented artists. Only 22, he and his group The Crickets had established themselves as one of the world's best-loved new acts during an 12-month period which had seen them score major international hits with songs like *That'll Be The Day, Rave On, Peggy Sue, Listen To Me* and *Oh Boy* - many written by Holly and members of The Crickets.

Although the recently-married Holly (real names Charles Hardin Holley) and the original Crickets no longer worked together, he had recruited musician friends from his home-town of Lubbock, Texas to form a new group for the tour. Many of his songs would become modern standards and continue to be recorded by some of the world's biggest stars to this day.

As a string of maudlin tribute records went into production, work began on compiling new collections of Buddy Holly albums, a process which the growth of CDs has helped maintain. It's a measure of his importance, especially in Britain, that everything Holly recorded during his two-year career is still available to modern-day fans.

The death of 17 year old Ritchie Valens was a severe blow to America's Mexican community, for which he had become a proud symbol through his hits *Come On Let's Go, Donna* and *La Bamba*. Like Holly, the Los Angeles-born Valens would become a source of inspiration for many younger performers, with his brief life made the subject of a major film.

Best known for his comedy hit *Chantilly Lace,* The Big Bopper - a larger-than-life figure and a popular disc jockey in Texas - was also a talented songwriter. He wrote the international hit *Running Bear* for Johnny Preston to hint at his potential.

Apartheid Architect Malan Dies

Spending the last four years of his life in austere retirement, Dr Daniel François Malan - a life-long fighter for white supremacy in South Africa, former prime minister and principal architect of the separate-race policy of apartheid - died today at his home in Stellenbosch, aged 84.

Educated partly at the University of Utrecht, Malan's close involvement with the Dutch Reformed Church led to his firm belief in Afrikaner nationalism and becoming, in 1918, a nationalist MP who served in the Herzog government, introduced measures to make Afrikaans an official language and tried to forcibly repatriate South Africa's Indian minority.

Leader of the opposition between 1934-39 and 1940-48, he opposed Jan Smuts' increased internationalism and South Africa's participation in WWII. Founder of a purified National Party, he became Prime Minister in 1948 and established apartheid as South Africa's new constitutional law. In 1952 his policies were held to be illegal by the South African Supreme Court - a judgement Malan countered by giving parliament the status of a High Court.

Malan retired in December 1954, handing over to Johannes Strijdom, an even more fanatical believer in apartheid.

Rhodesia: State Of Emergency Declared

Responding to what he claimed was the imminent threat of violence from black African nationalists, Rhodesian Prime Minister Sir Edgar Whitehead today declared a state of emergency, dissolved all African political parties and ordered the arrest of suspected ring-leaders and political dissidents.

A sweep by the British colony's police and military resulted in 435 immediate arrests - 88 per cent of those listed by the authorities. One of those who avoided capture was Joshua Nkomo, a key figure in the African nationalist movement. He was in Ghana for an All-Africa Peoples Conference.

It is generally accepted that Nkomo will not return to Rhodesia, but will lead the fight for political equality from the relative safety of exile.

UK TOP 10 SINGLES

1: As I Love You
- Shirley Bassey
2: One Night/I Got Stung
- Elvis Presley
3: Kiss Me Honey, Honey Kiss Me
- Shirley Bassey
4: Smoke Gets In Your Eyes
- The Platters
5: To Know Him Is To Love Him
- The Teddy Bears
6: Does Your Chewing Gum Lose Its Flavour
- Lonnie Donegan
7: Baby Face
- Little Richard
8: Problems
- The Everly Brothers
9: The Day The Rains Came
- Jane Morgan
10: (All Of A Sudden) My Heart Sings
- Paul Anka

FEBRUARY 21

Supermac Calls On Khrushchev At Kremlin

Now popularly known as 'Supermac' - a title inspired by political cartoonist Vicky's depiction of him in Superman-style cape and tights - British Prime Minister Harold Macmillan arrived in Moscow today for summit talks with Soviet leader Nikita Khrushchev.

During his 10-day stay, Macmillan would be a guest at Khrushchev's official dacha where their talks would focus on atomic arms reduction and the future of Berlin. Attracting headlines for wearing a traditional Russian-style sheepskin hat during his trip, Macmillan also visited Leningrad, Kiev, a number of museums and galleries, and was also shown around collective farms.

Joined near the end of his trip by Foreign Secretary Selwyn Lloyd, who had talks with his Soviet opposite number, Andrei Gromyko, Macmillan summarized his meetings with Khrushchev as 'a valuable exchange of views'. These included a general agreement to expand Anglo-Soviet trade and cultural ties.

Turkish Premier Survives Air Wreck To Sign Cyprus Peace Treaty

A PATIENT IN THE LONDON CLINIC since February 17, when he was injured in a Gatwick Airport crash which killed 12 of those aboard the *Viscount* airliner bringing him from Istanbul, Turkish Prime Minister Adnan Menderes was today able to add his signature to the agreement which set out the terms for an independent Cyprus and ended the bloody four-year civil war which had accounted for more than 500 deaths.

The deal, which also had the approval of Greek Cypriot leader Archbishop Makarios - based at London's posh Dorchester Hotel since his arrival from exile in Athens on February 17 - provided for Cyprus to become a republic within 12 months. Under the deal, Britain would be allowed to retain her two strategically-vital military bases on Cyprus and have wide ranging powers to react if they were threatened. But the treaty effectively spelled the end of 80 years of British rule, the last 34 years of which had seen Cyprus governed as a Crown Colony.

Forced into exile in March 1956, when he was forcibly put on a plane which took him initially to the Seychelles for a year of isolation before he was allowed to move to Athens, Archbishop Makarios would be given a hero's welcome when he finally returned to Cyprus on March 1. It was he who persuaded EOKA supporters to accept the peace treaty he'd negotiated and under which he planned to stand for election as the new republic's first president.

Age-Rule Change Gives Castro PM Title

Fidel Castro completed his astonishing sweep to power in Cuba today when he was sworn in as the country's new prime minister, a post he was only able to assume thanks to a change in Cuban election law.

Until February 11, the 30 year old guerrilla leader was too young to become prime minister or president, a title it is widely assumed he will eventually take. The solution was for the qualifying age to be reduced to 30, leaving the way clear for Castro to be elected unopposed and begin his task of building a new socialist utopia less than 100 miles from the US mainland of Florida.

It is there that thousands of former Batistá regime acolytes have begun building new lives for themselves and their families, and from where resistance to Castro will come in future years.

New Tube Line Planned For London

London Transport chiefs today unveiled details of a new addition to the city's underground train system, the 'Tube'.

To be called The Victoria Line, the new service will operate between the centre of the capital, at the mainline Victoria Station, and the north-east district of Walthamstow, which is currently not served by Tube services but is ideally placed to attract commuters from this heavily-populated part of the city.

Estimated to cost £50 million ($150m), the Victoria Line will be the first completely new addition to London Underground's network for 30 years. It is also planned to be much faster than existing lines, thanks to modern technology and new, more efficient trains.

MARCH 13

Report Blames Wing Ice For Busby Babes Air Tragedy

A BUILD-UP OF ICE on the wings of the BEA *Ambassador* which crashed while attempting to take off from Munich last February, was today blamed for the tragic accident which killed the cream of Manchester United's star-studded young team, nicknamed 'The Busby Babes' after their manager Matt Busby.

Eight members of the Manchester squad died in the crash, which happened as they were returning to England after beating Red Star Belgrade to win a place in the European Cup semi-finals. The death toll also included eight journalists who'd covered the game, and three members of the club's staff. A number of others were badly injured, including Busby himself (pictured with Bobby Charlton), who eventually recovered to begin re-building one of the world's most famous soccer clubs. The international level players who died included captain Roger Byrne, England's left-back since his 1954 debut, the 18-times England centre-forward Tommy Taylor, outside-left David Pegg (who'd won his first England cap in May 1957), Irish Republic inside-right Bill Whelan, and the outstanding English left-half Duncan Edwards. The other players killed were 21 year old right-half Eddie Colman, centre-half Mark Jones (24) and 25 year old Geoff Bent.

After landing at Munich to refuel, the BEA turbo-prop twice tried to take off on a snow-covered runway. During the second attempt it hit a fence and an airport building before breaking in two and bursting into flames.

According to today's official report, the weight of ice which had built up on the *Ambassador's* wings was too great to allow it to take off - something the pilot could not have known as he tried to get one of Europe's most formidable teams home.

Author Chandler Walks His Last Mean Street

Raymond Chandler, the master story-teller who created the classic tough-guy private eye Philip Marlowe and inspired hundreds of less-talented writers to flood the world's book stores with seedy, wise-cracking anti-heroes, died today at the age of 70.

Despite the ill-lit mean street settings of his most successful books, Chandler was an Englishman educated - like his contemporary PG Wodehouse - in the sedate academic groves of Dulwich College, in south London. A youthful contributor of essays and poems to English literary magazines, Chandler did not take up fiction writing until his mid-forties.

The Big Sleep, the first of only seven Philip Marlowe novels Chandler wrote after moving to California, was first published in 1939. Filmed in 1946, with Humphrey Bogart proving the definitive Marlowe, others which made it to the big screen included *Murder My Sweet, The Lady In The Lake, The Long Goodbye* and *The Blue Dahlia,* while Chandler's skills as a screenwriter were also used by Hollywood for the classic thrillers *Double Indemnity* and *Strangers On A Train.*

Chandler had tried to kill himself in 1955, after his wife died. His suicide attempt failed, like a twist in one of his beautifully crafted novels, when the cartridges he put in his revolver turned out to be damp!

Movie Comic Costello Bows Out

Lou Costello, the short, fat, put-upon half of comedy team Abbott and Costello, died in California today, only weeks after completing his first-ever solo movie, the remarkably titled mock-horror film *The Thirty-Foot Bride Of Candy Mountain.* He would have celebrated his fifty-third birthday on March 6.

Born Louis Cristillo, he formed a successful vaudeville team with the brusque and slightly shifty straight-man Bud Abbott in the 1930s. The couple made their first film in 1940, and until they called it a day in 1956 when Abbott decided he'd had enough, they made an average of two a year to establish themselves as one of Universal Studios' top stars and main money-makers.

While Abbott wheeled, dealed and bullied his way into and out of sticky situations, it was simple old Lou who got whacked with planks, custard pies and worse, invariably with a look of confused hurt which proved he didn't have a clue what was going on.

13

MARCH 9

EOKA Leader Grivas Retires As Greeks OK Cyprus Deal

Colonel George Grivas, the Greek army WWII hero who masterminded the murderous EOKA terrorist campaign which paralyzed Cyprus for close on four years, announced his retirement today as Greek Cypriot leaders agreed to accept the peace treaty signed in London last month by Archbishop Makarios and Adnan Menderes, the Turkish Prime Minister.

EOKA guerrillas attacked British military and civilian targets as well as the Turkish community, using guns, explosives and arson to harass the Mediterranean island state and try to win political union with Greece. Grivas successfully evaded capture throughout the campaign, despite a ceaseless manhunt and huge reward offers for his betrayal.

Allowed to leave Cyprus without being charged for any of the atrocities he'd ordered, Grivas would fly to Athens on March 17, where a huge crowd waited to greet him as a conquering hero.

MARCH 3

Senate Agrees To Accept Hawaii As US State

Hawaii, the Pacific Ocean island group which has been a US Territory since 1900, today learned that it is to become a fully-fledged part of the Union when the US Senate approved its application for statehood.

Formerly administered by Britain, when it was known as The British Sandwich Islands, Hawaii's strategic importance to the United States was confirmed on December 7, 1941 when a massive force of Japanese warplanes attacked the US Pacific Fleet moored in its home base of Pearl Harbor to bring America into WWII.

Disguised Dalai Lama Flees Chinese Regime In Tibet

THE DALAI LAMA, (pictured with his mother) spiritual leader of Tibet, the tiny Himalayan mountain country over-run by the Chinese in 1951 and scene of increasingly brutal suppression of an independence movement in recent months, was reported to be on his way to the Indian border today, his escape from the Tibetan capital of Lhasa made possible by warriors of the fierce Khamba tribe. Travelling in a train of mules and yaks, the Dalai Lama was said to be disguised as a servant.

Extensive fighting was reported around rebel forts along the Dalai Lama's escape route, while Chinese paratroops were dropped into the region between the Brahmaputra River and the Indian border in a bid to capture him before he reached the frontier. They had strict orders to take him alive - the Dalai Lama's death would trigger a nationwide uprising even the Chinese would find it nearly impossible to contain.

A total of 9,000 Tibetans loyal to the Dalai Lama would eventually join him in his flight to safety, leaving a country viewed as a mere province by the communist government in Beijing. They have been ruthless in their treatment of the civilian population and ferocious in their punishment of nationalist fighters captured in battle.

China has had an unexpected bonus in the defection of the Panchen Lama, Tibet's second-highest spiritual figurehead. He is known to have contacted Chinese leader Mao Tse-tung, congratulating his forces on what he called their 'tremendous victory' in suppressing resistance.

BEN-HUR TURNS OSCARS NIGHT INTO CLEAN SWEEP FOR HESTON AND CO

The sand-and-sandals epic *Ben-Hur* confirmed its position as the movie industry's safest bet for years when it won a record-breaking (and still unbeaten) 11 Oscars for just about everyone involved in its creation - from director William Wyler, leading man Charlton Heston and the irrepressible Welsh actor Hugh Griffith, to the art direction team, the editors, the main cameraman, the costume designer, composer Miklos Rosza, the sound technicians and the special effects wizards who helped convinced us that the legendary chariot race really did take place in an arena packed with 10,000 screaming punters.

As is invariably the way, the Academy of Motion Pictures Arts and Sciences managed to come up with its fair share of puzzles in its final short-lists of nominations.

While *Ben-Hur* beat *Anatomy Of A Murder, The Diary Of Anne Frank, The Nun's Story* and *Room At The Top* to take the Best Picture prize, there was no nomination for *Some Like It Hot* even though Billy Wilder was justly included in the Best Director section!

Strangely, while Jack Lemmon (*Some Like It Hot*) found himself in competition with Heston (*Ben Hur*), Laurence Harvey (for *RoomAt The Top*), Paul Muni (for *The Last Angry Man*) and James Stewart (*Anatomy Of A Murder*) for the Best Actor trophy, his excellent co-star, Tony Curtis, didn't even rate a mention.

The gritty British drama *Room At The Top,* a runaway international hit this year, scored an impressive six nominations. In the event, it won only two - for Simone Signoret, who beat Doris Day (*Pillow Talk*), Audrey Hepburn (*The Nun's Story*), Elizabeth Taylor and Katharine Hepburn (both for *Suddenly, Last Summer*) to take the Best Actress Oscar, and screenwriter Neil Paterson, who adapted John Braine's best-selling novel to such great effect.

Greatest applause of the night, however, was reserved for the silent comedy genius Buster Keaton, awarded an honorary Oscar for his remarkable contribution to movies long before the industry decided to have an annual party to give each other prizes for making more money than is generally thought decent by us mere mortals.

*Marilyn Monroe and Tony Curtis
Some Like It Hot*

Castro Woos US Press, Denies He's A Commie

Dressed in the distinctive battle fatigues which appear to have become his trademark dress style, victorious Cuban rebel-turned-prime minister Fidel Castro spent today trying to persuade American political leaders and opinion-makers that his new regime does not constitute a communist threat. In Washington DC on an 11-day visit to discuss the future of US bases on Cuba, Castro assured Congressional leaders that the mutual US-Cuban defence treaties would be honoured in full, with the key US Navy base at Guantanamo Bay being allowed to continue operations.

Speaking tonight at a dinner given by the influential American Society of Newspaper Editors, the 32 year old drew warm applause from his high-powered audience when he told them firmly: 'We are not communists!'

Dalai Lama Reaches India

Thousands of Tibetan exiles packed the rail station in the West Bengal town of Siliguri today to stage an emotional welcome for their spiritual leader, the Dalai Lama, who managed to evade Chinese forces and cross the Tibet-India border at Assam yesterday. Greeted by tearful relatives as Tibetan music blared from station loudspeakers, the young fugitive received a long line of officials before taking his place on a blue and white striped dais to accept the traditional Tibetan greeting-offering of white silk scarves. So many were thrown by his overjoyed compatriots, reporters described the air over the Dalai Lama as resembling a white mist.

NASA Picks Team With The Right Stuff

NASA, THE NATIONAL Aeronautics and Space Administration created last year by President Eisenhower to mastermind America's faltering space programme, today announced the names of the USAAF test pilots selected to take part in Project Mercury, its bid to beat the Soviet Union's plan to put a man into orbit.

The seven men - all married, and all in their thirties - are (pictured left to right) Walter Schirra, Alan Shepard, Virgil Grissom, Donald Slayton, John Glenn, Scott Carpenter and Gordon Cooper. Picked from the cream of US military pilots who had volunteered to join NASA, they were to receive no extra payment for what is generally considered hazardous duty.

NASA was formed last July after President Eisenhower decided the United States' previous military-led and administered space agency needed an injection of civilian expertise to compete better with a Soviet programme which had already successfully launched two satellites and a dog into space. Many qualified scientists and physicists were known to be reluctant to work for military bosses, or lend their skills to a programme which could be highjacked for arms race applications.

With the USSR claiming that its next objective was to put a man into space, NASA was quick to begin recruiting boffins from all over the world, and just as quick to start finding men who had the right stuff to give the US a chance to beat the Russians.

UK TOP 10 SINGLES

1: Side Saddle
- Russ Conway
2: It Doesn't Matter Anymore
- Buddy Holly
3: Smoke Gets In Your Eyes
- The Platters
4: Petite Fleur
- Chris Barber's Jazz Band
5: My Happiness
- Connie Francis
6: Stagger Lee
- Lloyd Price
7: Donna
- Marty Wilde
8: As I Love You
- Shirley Bassey
9: Gigi
- Billy Eckstine
10: Charlie Brown
- The Coasters

APRIL 22

Decoy Duck Role For Swan-Like Ballerina Fonteyn

IMPLICATED IN a plot that wouldn't disgrace a James Bond adventure, prima ballerina Dame Margot Fonteyn arrived in New York tonight to face a barrage of press questions about her part in the failed coup attempted in Panama by her husband, Dr Roberto Arias, the central American republic's former Ambassador to London. He was still being hunted in Panama while Dame Margot - having spent a night in jail answering police questions - had been allowed to leave when her protestations of innocence were believed.

Looking tired, but none the worse for her adventure, the 39 year old Covent Garden dancer managed to avoid answering journalists' most pressing questions with a cheerful self-possession. She was, however, able to confirm the few facts which had leaked out of Panama.

According to Panamanian authorities, Dr Arias was suspected of planning a Cuban-aided coup, timed to coincide with a one-day state visit by Prince Philip, who had arrived aboard the royal yacht *Britannia*.

With his internationally-famous wife providing cover for his actions, Dr Arias was said to have stocked a launch with rifles, revolvers, machine guns and grenades in preparation. It was this craft Panamanian police seized after a tip-off. With her husband a fugitive, they held Dame Margot until she convinced them that she knew nothing.

Referring to one of her most acclaimed roles, in *Swan Lake*, Britain's shadow Foreign Secretary Aneurin Bevan, raised smiles in the House of Commons when he said the British public did not appreciate 'having seen her in the role of the swan, seeing her in the role of a decoy duck'.

The Cuban connection in the Arias plot appeared to be confirmed only nine days later when a small force of Cuban troops who'd landed secretly in Panama surrendered after their presence became known and they were surrounded by Panamanian soldiers.

Work Starts On Cockerell's Hovercraft

First unveiled last year as a set of technical drawings and a small working model, the new *Hovercraft* invented by Suffolk boat builder Christopher Cockerell took a step nearer reality today when work began on a first two-ton craft at the Saunders Roe shipyard on the Isle of Wight.

A revolutionary concept in amphibious vehicles, Cockerell's *Hovercraft* is designed to be able to travel over land and sea on a cushion of air trapped beneath a flexible rubber 'apron'. With backing from the government-supported National Research and Development Corporation, the first completed *Hovercraft* is scheduled to begin trials in June. Among the long-term plans for *Hovercraft* are a 100-ton model capable of carrying passengers and a 1,000-ton freight version.

Chalk Marks Halt British Shipyard

Inter-union warfare brought Cammell Laird, one of Britain's biggest shipyards, to a halt today as workers argued over which union's members had the right to draw a simple chalk mark.

Nearly 2,000 men were laid off when Boilermakers' Society members walked out after discovering that a shipwright had been given the job of marking where a steel plate should be cut. This was traditionally a boilermaker's role when plates were cut on shore, but they are now cut on board ship to save time.

While their employers have refused to get involved in the dispute, they have warned that the strike threatens to harm the yard's image and damage prospects of future orders. The strike would drag on until July, when the Trades Union Congress told the boilermakers to return to work.

MAY

MAY 30

Work Begins On Mont Blanc Tunnel

While British engineers were busy using the moon to link up with America (see separate story), French engineers today began work on a project aimed at ending the more down-to-earth problem which had vexed untold generations of people who lived on either side of Mont Blanc but were unable to reach each other for long periods during winter, when snow and ice made the roads and tracks linking them impassable. A dramatic increase in road freight and car traffic since the end of WWII forced authorities in France and Italy to combine forces and finances to embark on one of the biggest civil engineering projects of modern times.

When it was finally opened in August 1962, the Mont Blanc Tunnel would completely transform vital communications between the two nations, and provide a new and safer crossing point for Swiss motorists for whom it also offered a transformation in winter driving.

MAY 27

British Smokers Take A Tip From Health Warnings

Advised and warned for the past two years that their habit could increase their chances of contracting cancer, British cigarette smokers do not appear to have reduced their consumption of the dreaded weed. What they have done, according to figures released in London today, is switch to brands with filter tips. The Tobacco Manufacturers' standing committee annual report showed that sales of filtered cigarettes in Britain rose from £10.1 million ($30.3m) in 1957, to more than £18 million ($54m) in 1958. Overall tobacco sales continued to rise, however - from 1957's reported £256 million ($768m) to last year's £260.8 million ($782.4m).

MAY 24

US Loses John Foster Dulles, Cold War Warrior

JOHN FOSTER DULLES, the 71 year old maverick Secretary of State who once threatened to use the atomic bomb to halt Soviet aggression and made repeated calls for the West to liberate Russian-controlled Eastern Europe, died today after a two-year fight with cancer. He had resigned only five weeks ago.

A principal architect of American Cold War policy and tactics, Dulles' unrelenting hatred of communism is believed by many to have denied the West the chance to negotiate advantageous settlements at crucial times. However, there is little doubt that same inflexible approach was crucial in helping maintain Western unity in fighting the Cold War.

A committed Christian, Dulles was educated at Princeton and in Paris before establishing himself as a successful lawyer in New York. His deep understanding of international affairs led to President Eisenhower appointing him Secretary of State in 1953, and a formidable first-year schedule which saw him visit 40 countries, build up NATO and create the South-East Asia Treaty Organization (SEATO) to link Australia, the US, Britain, France, New Zealand, Pakistan, Thailand and the Philippines in a collective action pact aimed at resisting communist aggression or communist-inspired internal subversion.

Relations between the US and Britain were strained by Dulles' inability to collaborate with British PM Sir Anthony Eden, and his opposition to the Anglo-French attempts to seize the Suez Canal in 1956 helped ensure its failure and Eden's inevitable resignation.

Hancock Starts Last Series Of Half-Hour Classics

Britain amended its evening social diaries again this month as the fourth annual series of *Hancock's Half Hour* - for the past three years the BBC's most popular programme - returned to capture its top spot in the national TV ratings.

Starring former radio star Tony Hancock and regular side-kick Sid James - destined to find even wider fame as lynchpin of the Carry On films - this would turn out to be the last series the comedian would make with James. When he returned in 1961, the show would be simply retitled *Hancock* and produce such comedy classics as the timeless Blood Donor and Radio Ham episodes. Written by Ray Galton and Alan Simpson, *Hancock's Half Hour* developed the pompous loser character who lived in genteel poverty and a haze of grandiose - and inevitably frustrated - schemes in the fictional South London suburb of East Cheam. At his peak, Anthony Aloysius St. John Hancock decimated British pub takings on the nights his misadventures were broadcast.

UK TOP 10 SINGLES

1: A Fool Such As I
/I Need Your Love Tonight
- Elvis Presley
2: It Doesn't Matter Anymore
- Buddy Holly
3: Side Saddle
- Russ Conway
4: Donna
- Marty Wilde
5: It's Late
- Ricky Nelson
6: Petite Fleur
- Chris Barber's Jazz Band
7: I've Waited So Long
- Anthony Newley
8: Come Softly To Me
- The Fleetwoods
9: Charlie Brown
- The Coasters
10: Come Softly To Me
- Frankie Vaughan
& The Kaye Sisters

MAY 6

Britain Protests At Iceland's 'Cod War' Actions

A NUMBER OF RECENT near-collisions and close-shave shellings led the British government to lodge an official protest with the Icelandic government today, accusing the Reykjavik authorities of employing increasingly violent tactics against British trawlers in what the British press have begun calling 'The Cod War'.

The year-old argument between the two countries was a simple case of Iceland trying to reduce and restrict the amount of fish being taken by British trawlers out of what it considered traditional Icelandic fishing waters, even though the area in dispute lay outside Iceland's internationally-recognized 12-mile administrative limit.

The British note, delivered to the Icelandic Foreign Ministry in Reykjavic,

protested at the 'dangerous manoeuvres' of the coastguard ship Maria Julia, which had almost collided with the British destroyer Contest a week earlier. Its main criticism was aimed at Iceland's decision to arm its gunboats with live shells to drive off UK-based trawlers. This had led to the most serious incident yet, when one of 20 live rounds fired at the Hull fishing boat Arctic Viking missed by only three yards. The confrontation ended when the British vessel turned towards the gunboat, which retreated. Describing the actions of Icelandic ships as 'dangerous and unseamanlike', the British protest said they went beyond any measures designed merely to identify the British boats involved, the Icelandic defence for its activities.

MAY 15

Moon Used To Link Britain and US

The age of communications satellites being some years off, physicists at Britain's newly-opened Jodrell Bank radio telescope in Cheshire decided to use the next most obvious space object when they attempted to send radio messages to scientists in the United States today.

Aiming their transmitters at the moon, they successfully bounced clear signals to their American colleagues. Until science came up with a more satisfactory and controllable solution, they now knew of a novel way of stretching communications links even further.

New Cases Confirm US North-South Race Divide

The gap between conservative southern US states determined to maintain white supremacy, and the more liberal equal-rights movement trying to enforce Supreme Court judgements which have outlawed segregation, was confirmed as being as wide as ever this month.

On May 22, Alabama state authorities proved just how deep their bigotry could be when they banned the sale of a children's book which featured the marriage of a black rabbit and a white rabbit.

The Supreme Court played its part on May 25 when it ruled that a Louisiana law which banned mixed-race boxing matches was unconstitutional.

Able And Baker Orbit To Aid US Space Research

MAY 28

Two monkeys returned safely to earth today after a 1,700 mile round trip which put them 360 miles above the surface. Their flight, inside a *Jupiter* missile nose cone, marked the first successful American launch and return of live animals, with the resulting information considered vital to NASA's much-vaunted plan to be the first to put a man into space.

The animals - Able, a seven-pound rhesus monkey, and Baker, a one-pound squirrel monkey - were picked up from the Atlantic by a US Navy ship. During their trip they were monitored to find how they were affected by the incredible acceleration and deceleration of take-off and re-entry, by weightlessness while in space, and the overall stress of their experience. NASA delight at the mission's success was dampened on June 2 when Able died during an operation to remove an electrode from his brain.

Audience Vote BBC-TV's Juke Box Jury A Hit

The BBC picked a winner today with the first-ever edition of Juke Box Jury, a new pop music show destined to become an instant hit with TV viewers and a firm favourite for almost 10 years.

The format, devised by Peter Potter, had disc jockey David Jacobs presiding over the views of four panellists subjected to a selection of that week's new singles. They had to say whether they thought they'd be hits or misses, and why. An air of tension was guaranteed by the fact that every show had at least one artist hiding behind a screen listening to the jury's opinions and ready to confront anyone who'd been especially rude about their latest pride and joy. First four occupants of the hot seats were DJ Pete Murray, singers Alma Cogan and Gary Miller, and 'typical teenager' Susan Stranks, later to gain fame as presenter of the children's TV show Magpie. On one famous future occasion, the four-man jury would be John, Paul, George and Ringo - The Beatles.

De Valéra Becomes Irish President

Eamonn de Valéra took another giant step into history today at Dublin Castle when he took the oath of office in a simple ceremony which made him the new President of the Irish Republic. Now aged 76, he was effectively moving from the heart of political influence into a strictly non-political and largely ceremonial role.

The New York born veteran stunned members of Fianna Fail - the party he founded in 1926 with a core of staunch republicans who had, like him, been jailed by the British in their victorious struggle for Irish independence - when he announced his resignation earlier this year.

Popularly known as 'The Chief', de Valéra built Fianna Fail into Ireland's most effective political administrative machine and enjoyed 21 years as a prime minister used to making all major decisions himself.

Johansson Floors Floyd To Take Title To Sweden

SWEDISH AND EUROPEAN boxing champ Ingemar Johansson - who was shamefully disqualified during the second round of the Helsinki Olympic Games final in 1952 for 'not fighting' - took less than three full rounds to stun the boxing world, an astonished and disbelieving Yankee Stadium crowd, and title-holder Floyd Patterson (pictured) tonight in New York when he became the first non-American to become world heavyweight champion since Italy's Primo Carnera 25 years ago.

The Swede, whose right hand punch he called 'The Hammer of God', entered the fight with two great advantages - the champion's complacency and an apparent lack of American awareness of his formidable punching power, despite his one-round KO of American Eddie Machen, the No.1 contender, in Gothenburg last year.

Deliberately playing up the playboy image projected by his manager, Johansson was written off by US sports writers, who had to re-think their pre-composed headlines when the Swede knocked Patterson down seven times in the third round before the referee stepped in.

JUNE 23

Soviet Spy Fuchs Freed, Goes East

Klaus Fuchs, the top nuclear scientist imprisoned by a British court in 1950 after being found guilty of passing British and American atom secrets to the Russians, walked free today and said he intended to live in East Germany, his country of birth.

Fuchs was arrested in Britain following an FBI tip to the British secret service. He'd spent seven years working in British and US research bases, during which time he passed information to Soviet agents to save the Russians years of work.

Working at the Harwell weapons research centre in Berkshire when arrested, Fuchs admitted his treason and to being a life-long communist, but said he had ceased spying a year earlier.

JUNE 23

Transplants Lead To London 'Spare Parts' Bank

With most skin, bone and cornea transplant problems solved by the world's most brilliant surgeons, plans were announced in London today to create the world's first 'bank' of much-needed body parts, including livers and kidneys.

The facility is to be based at London's Hammersmith Hospital, but its vital stock could be used for patients at other British or European hospitals, and may prove the foundation of a global transplant supply service in the long-term. The Hammersmith centre will involve the modification of a heart-lung machine developed by David Melrose which the hospital authorities confirmed will enable a kidney transplant next year. At present a complete organ transplant had only been achieved between twins.

JUNE 26

Queen And Ike Open St.Lawrence Seaway

Hundreds of thousands of Americans and Canadians crowded the Quebec town of St Lambert today as Queen Elizabeth and President Eisenhower (pictured) inaugurated the St Lawrence Seaway, the massive canal and locks system which finally allowed deep-draught, ocean-going ships to reach the Great Lakes from the Atlantic. Of immense commercial value to both nations, the project linked Montreal and Lake Ontario and gave their industrial heartlands greater access to the world's trading centres.

American and Canadian engineers worked on the Seaway for almost five years. Fittingly, as he had taken great personal interest in the project, the huge complex of gates on the New York State side of the eastern entrance to the Seaway was given the name Eisenhower Locks.

South African Women Lead Black Slum Clearance Riots

LED BY SEVERAL THOUSAND angry women, more than 50,000 black South Africans joined in running battles with armed police in the slum township of Cato Manor today. They were protesting against plans to demolish the settlement and a recently introduced ban on home-brewed beer.

During the riots - which many men joined only after being driven from beer halls by stick-wielding women - houses, beer halls, offices and cars were burned. The worst damage only stopped when police began firing warning shots into the air with Sten guns before attacking rioters with whips, batons and clubs.

The riots were sparked by the South African government's decision to bulldoze Capo Manor - one of the racially-divided country's most notorious slums - before plans to build a new township were completed. This meant that most of the township's inhabitants would be temporarily homeless and face the additional risks of compulsory removal back to tribal homelands, complete lack of work prospects and probable poverty and starvation.

MECKIFF ACTION CONTROVERSY SOURS WINTER TEST SERIES

A test match series between England and Australia would not be complete without at least one controversy to add an edge to what is anyway a traditionally edgy meeting of old enemies. This year it came during England's tour Down Under, when the action of Australian fast left-arm bowler Ian Meckiff was questioned during the second Test in Melbourne.

The fact that England's batsmen collapsed under the second innings attack launched by Meckiff (who took six wickets for only 38 runs) and Alan Davidson (3-41) to record their lowest score in Australia for 55 years, obviously had nothing to do with the mutterings that came from various old buffers, and would continue to come until Meckiff bowed out of the international scene in 1963. The rules governing a bowler's action are designed to eliminate the possibility of throwing, and Meckiff's unusual approach meant he came running in with his arm apparently bent until the very last moment, when it straightened and the ball left his fingers with obviously effective venom.

For the record, Australia won the series 4-1, regaining the Ashes they'd lost in England in 1953. They did it using a technically excellent squad of young players led by Richie Benaud, who simply out-played, out-thought and out-did an ageing English team in real need of a transfusion of enthusiasm and verve. Benaud's overall contribution to Australia's victory was typified by his wicket tally of 5-91 and 4-82, and his 46 runs in the first innings of his team's win in the final Test in Adelaide.

REAL CONTINUE TO DOMINATE THE EUROPEAN CUP

Already victors of the first three European Cup finals by beating Stade de Reims 4-3 in 1956, Fiorentina 2-0 in 1957 and Madrid 3-2 last year in Brussels, the mighty Real Madrid faced French champions Reims again in Stuttgart this year, with more than 67,000 fans anxious to see if the Spanish supremos could maintain their unbelievable record.

They could. Thanks to unanswered goals by their superstar centre-forward skipper, the Argentinian-born Alfredo Di Stefano, and Mateos, Real Madrid saw their name carved on the trophy for the fourth time.

In England, Manchester United began their climb back from the horrors of the 1958 Munich air crash. Coached once more by a now-recovered Matt Busby, they managed to end the 1958-59 First Division season as runners-up to Wolverhampton Wanderers.

Nottingham Forest won the FA Cup by beating Luton 2-1, while the Scottish season saw Glasgow Rangers shave the league championship from Hearts, who gained some satisfaction by beating Partick Thistle 5-1 to take the Scottish League Cup. St. Mirren faced Aberdeen in the Scottish FA Cup final, emerging 3-1 winners.

A memorable career landmark for England soccer captain Billy Wright as he led his team out of the Wembley Stadium tunnel to face Scotland on April 11- and so become the first player in history to win 100 international caps.

The 35 year old Wolverhampton Wanderers central defender had his enjoyment completed with the Bobby Charlton goal which ensured England's victory over 'the old enemy'. As the final whistle sounded, Wright's team-mates raised him shoulder high to take a well-deserved lap of honour.

BRABHAM PUSHES HIS LUCK TO TAKE FORMULA 1 TITLE

With Juan Fangio retired and reigning world champion Mike Hawthorn tragically killed in a motoring accident, the 1959 Formula 1 racing season seemed to offer Britain's Stirling Moss a great chance of finally getting his hands on the coveted World Championship. It didn't turn out that way.

Offered rides by just about every major works team, Moss elected to drive for the Scottish-based Rob Walker outfit, using a Climax-powered Cooper. Ironically, Moss would face eventual defeat at the hands of Australian Jack Brabham, who helped engineer John Cooper produce the Cooper team's new T51. Like the Walker team's 'old' Cooper, Brabham's beast had a Coventry-Climax engine.

Although Moss won the Portuguese and Italian Grands Prix, he was forced to retire from the Monaco and Dutch meetings with gearbox trouble. Brabham won the Monaco and registered enough good finishes in other events for the season's final race – the US Grand Prix at Sebring, Florida, to be the clincher. Simply, if Moss finished in the points he'd be champion. If Brabham failed to win any points and Ferrari's Tony Brooks won, it would be a tie between Moss and Brabham. Just as simply, Moss was forced to retire in lap 10, Brabham ran out of fuel in the last lap and, although he was overtaken by the eventual race winner, Bruce McLaren, Stirling Moss's team-mate Maurice Trintignant and Brooks, he literally pushed his car over the line to take fourth place – and the World Championship.

Billy Wright, chaired by R Clayton and D Howe, after becoming the first player in history to win 100 international caps

JULY 17

Lady Day Billie Sings Her Last Blues

ONE OF THE GREATEST VOICES IN JAZZ was stilled today when Billie Holiday (pictured), the singer who sang blues based on the experience of a life of professional and personal battles, failed affairs and long periods of heroin addiction, died at the age of 44.

Popularly and affectionately known to the jazz world as 'Lady Day', she was born Eleanora Fagan, the illegitimate daughter of teenage parents, in Baltimore. Viciously raped at the age of ten, she became a prostitute in her mid-teens. Moving to New York with her mother in 1929, Holiday began singing in Harlem clubs and soon came to the attention of jazz producer John Hammond, who set her on the road to stardom with a series of recordings which revealed a glorious black voice which - unlike most of her contemporaries - made no effort to sound white.

Holiday spent the 1930s working with some of the best players in jazz, including Duke Ellington, Benny Goodman, Count Basie, Oscar Peterson and Lester Young. While she made some timeless recordings - including *Good Morning Heartache*, *The Man I Love*, *All Of Me*, *Strange Fruit*, *God Bless The Child* and *Why Was I Born?* - increasing problems with alcohol and drugs took their toll on the voice and professional reputation of the star who'd adopted the distinctive on-stage trademark of a white gardenia tucked into her hair.

By the 1940s, above-par Holiday performances were rare, and recordings made in the early 1950s reveal a tortured, rasping and tragic travesty of the voice that had once captivated millions.

Arrested and jailed for narcotics possession in 1948, Holiday died at Metropolitan Hospital, New York where she'd been detained pending further possession charges. Still an abiding influence on women jazz singers to this day, Holiday's life was portrayed movingly on film by Diana Ross in the 1973 movie *Lady Sings The Blues*.

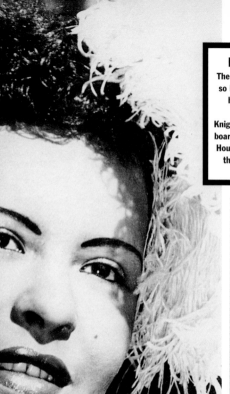

Harrods Take-Over War Hots Up

The battle for ownership of Harrods, the swanky London store so beloved of the world's richest and most famous shoppers, hotted up today when The House of Fraser stores group launched a take-over bid to counter that of Harrods Knightsbridge neighbour, Debenham's. Aware that the Harrods board favoured last month's relatively-friendly Debenham's bid, House of Fraser press releases went to great lengths to stress that the group would not tamper with the top shop's style, philosophy or dedication to exclusivity.

Commons Furore Over African Death Camps

The British government faced a sustained and vitriolic attack of its foreign policies in the House of Commons today, with the strongest calls for resignation coming during exchanges about the deaths of 51 Africans during riots in Nyasaland and 11 more in a Kenyan prison camp.

The row, probably the worst to greet the government since the Suez Crisis in 1956, came as Colonial Secretary Alan Lennox-Boyd attempted to defend Britain's rule of its ever-shrinking empire, most especially African colonies split by guerrilla-backed independence movements.

Armed with the recent findings of a judicial inquiry into the deaths of the 51 Nyasaland rioters, which criticized the actions of security forces, and continued controversy over the ways in which 11 Mau Mau detainees died in Kenya, Labour MPs accused the Conservatives of attempting to whitewash massacres and called for fresh talks to be held with those seeking independence from Britain.

UK TOP 10 SINGLES

1: **Dream Lover**
- Bobby Darin
2: **Battle Of New Orleans**
- Lonnie Donegan
3: **A Teenager In Love**
- Marty Wilde
4: **Roulette**
- Russ Conway
5: **Peter Gunn Theme**
- Duane Eddy
6: **Personality**
- Anthony Newley
7: **Living Doll**
- Cliff Richard
8: **A Fool Such As I / I Need Your Love Tonight**
- Elvis Presley
9: **Goodbye Jimmy, Goodbye**
- Ruby Murray
10: **It's Late**
- Ricky Nelson

JULY 25

Khrushchev And Nixon In Hot Kitchen Debate

AN AMERICAN KITCHEN IN Moscow became the unlikely setting for one of the most heated and unscripted confrontations of the Cold War today when Soviet leader Nikita Khrushchev and US Vice-President Richard Nixon (pictured) exchanged frank views on everything from the merits of washing machines to nuclear strategy and foreign policy.

To no-one's great surprise, the couple managed to find very little common ground, although Khrushchev was guardedly impressed by the display of energy-saving gadgets arrayed in the 'typical' American kitchen, part of a US trade exhibition in the Russian capital.

The two men - one the acknowledged leader of the communist world, the other a long-avowed enemy of state socialism - were on what was intended to be little more than a brief official tour of the exhibition. It turned into an impromptu summit when Nixon tried to steer Khrushchev into the kitchen and an initially dismissive Russian was tempted to get a closer look at the electrical appliances.

For the next hour the two stood in deep and often heated conversation as reporters and photographers fought to catch snatches of what all agreed to call 'The Kitchen Debate'. With their interpreters working overtime, Nixon and Khrushchev argued the merits of communism and capitalism, their respective foreign policies, the nuclear arms

race, and the real value of food processors over old-fashioned elbow grease.

While it is not known what Khrushchev made of the confrontation with the man who would one day become President of the United States, Nixon's 1978 memoirs recalled that it ended with both men swearing that, despite their differences, all they wanted was peace.

Radio Veteran Greene To Head BBC

The BBC kept faith with its own today when the board of governors announced that the organization's next Director-General was to be Hugh Carleton Green, brother of the author Graham Greene and the BBC's present head of news and current affairs. Greene was to succeed Sir Ian Trevor, Director-General for the past seven years, and would be paid £8,000 ($24,000) a year to run an ever-expanding network of services facing the double challenge of changing public tastes and an explosion of new communications technology in both television and radio.

A former journalist, Greene was chief German correspondent for The Daily Telegraph until 1939. He joined the BBC after war service with the Royal Air Force.

Castro Takes Over Cuban Presidency

Cuba's new guard assumed full political control over the island state today when Prime Minister Fidel Castro orchestrated the resignation of Dr Manuel Urrutia, President since Castro's overwhelming military victory over the now-exiled President Batistá in January, and took the oath of office to emerge as undisputed supremo of the new socialist republic.

On July 12 Castro had protested that the US was meddling in Cuban affairs by granting political asylum to a former air force chief accused of corruption. It was widely believed that President Urrutia's reluctance to add his voice to the protest meant he had to go.

St Laurent: Hemlines Up! Chanel: Let Them Down!

The world of high fashion was thrown into turmoil today in Paris when the two most influential designers, Dior's Yves St Laurent and Coco Chanel, unveiled new collections which offered completely contradictory ideas on the length of skirts.

For St Laurent, who had made his dislike of knees well known in the past, it was a case of volte face. His collection, clearly aimed at younger women, was packed with puffed above-the-knee skirts and models resplendent in high, bouffant hairstyles. Critics dismissed the look, suggesting it was little more than fancy dress and signalled the beginning of the end for the House of Dior.

Coco Chanel led most of the rest by dropping the hemlines of her now-classic tailored suits. She also paid tribute to one of her most famous clients by using models whose features and hair matched the waif-like style of the elfin actress Audrey Hepburn.

AUG

Arkansas Whites Protest Little Rock School Integration

MORE THAN 20 WHITE demonstrators were arrested in the Arkansas state capital of Little Rock today as police fought with about 200 segregationists trying to stop black students enrolling at the city's Central High School. The protest was almost a carbon copy of events in September 1957 when President Eisenhower sent National Guardsmen to Little Rock to enforce a Supreme Court ruling that educational segregation in southern schools was illegal.

Earlier, a crowd of 1,000 whites had held a dawn vigil on the steps of the State Capitol, where Governor Orval Faubus told them: 'I am with you all the way'. A rabid segregationist, Faubus ordered a number of Arkansas schools closed in 1957 rather than comply with the integration edict.

The splinter group arrived at Central High just before the first two black students - Elizabeth Eckford and Jefferson Thomas - entered the building. Police were forced to use truncheons and fire hoses to keep the mob at bay, and the arrests were made on demonstrators who either used violence in their bid to stop the students, or refused to obey orders to leave the area.

AUGUST 9

Ooh La La! Les Halles To Move

Paris city council stunned the world and outraged many of its citizens today when it announced it planned to close Les Halles, the city's ancient central market, and build a new, modern version on the outskirts.

The site of a market for almost 800 years, Les Halles was considered too old, too inefficient and too expensive to maintain. While conservationists and architectural historians began huffing and puffing over what they described as sheer vandalism, people living in the narrow ancient streets which have become a traffic controller's nightmare raised a quiet cheer.

Not cheering were the hundreds of, erm, ladies of the night for whom Les Halles was a regular haunt and a vital source of income. If the all-night cafés closed, and lonely businessmen stopped dropping by, they were going to have to start finding new 'digs' to continue playing their part in the Parisian leisure industry.

AUGUST 24

It's Hugh Fraser, By Appointment

Hugh Fraser, the accountant who stepped into the Harrods take-over tussle last month, was today celebrating success in his bid to own the posh London emporium proud to say its services are By Appointment to HM Queen Elizabeth II.

The Harrods board conceded that House of Fraser, the group of companies headed by the Scottish entrepreneur and already owner of a number of department stores, had acquired enough shares to defeat the bid by Debenham's, the store group which opened the battle and with whom Harrods would have preferred to do business.

AUGUST 31

Tonight, From London: The Ike 'n' Mac Show!

British politics entered the television age with a vengeance tonight when President Eisenhower and Prime Minister Harold Macmillan appeared live from Downing Street, taking part in what appeared to be a relaxed and unrehearsed conversation.

Cynics were quick to point out that the broadcast, a notable first for the BBC and the two leaders, would probably do much to enhance Macmillan's image as a world statesman only weeks before it was thought he'd call a general election. This view was reinforced by the route taken by Ike's motorcade from London Airport four days earlier - a zig-zag course which allowed huge cheering crowds in marginal constituencies to catch a glimpse of the former Supreme Commander of Allied Forces as he returned for a five-day visit 'to the land I love'.

ARRIVALS

Born this month:

1: Joe Elliott, UK rock singer (Def Leppard)

10: Rosanna Arquette, US TV and film actress (*Desperately Seeking Susan, After Hours,* etc);

12: Lynette Woodard, US basketball star (Olympic gold 1984), first female Harlem Globetrotter 1985

14: Earvin 'Magic' Johnson, US and Olympic basketball superstar *(see Came & Went pages)*

21: Anne Hobbs, UK tennis player

23: Edwin Collins, UK pop singer, songwriter (Orange Juice)

27: Gerhard Berger, Austrian Formula 1 racing star

29: Eddi Reader, UK pop singer, songwriter (Fairground Attraction)

DEPARTURES

Died this month:

6: Preston Sturges, US Oscar-winning film director, screenwriter

21: Sir Jacob Epstein, British sculptor, artist *(see Came & Went pages)*

Birth Of The Mini, The Biggest Little Car

DESTINED TO RIVAL THE E-TYPE Jag as the epitome of British style in the Swinging Sixties and the VW Beetle as the favourite runaround of young trendies, the British Motor Corporation's *Mini* took its first bow today when Alec Issigonis, the brilliant Italian-born designer responsible for the small wonder, was given the honour of unveiling it to British and European motoring writers.

In fact he unveiled two *Minis*, for BMC decided to make both Austin and Morris versions, though the only difference lay in a slightly different front-end look.

In all other respects, those invited to test drive the little newcomer found a compact four-seater (though future generations of students would dispute that!) which was surprisingly roomy. Issigonis and his team had achieved that by placing the four small wheels on the corners and mounting the engine - capable of cruising at 70 mph - sideways.

Styling was minimal, with sparse instrumentation, pull-strings to open the two doors, and sliding front door windows. The body was also basic and practical, with exposed door hinges. But with a purchase-tax-included price tag of only £500, the Mini was a snip

Barclays Enter The Computer Age

Barclays Bank, the British-owned international financial house, today announced that it had decided to order a computer - the first in the country to take the plunge into what many predict is the technology of the future.

The American giant IBM have agreed to supply Barclays with a large mainframe computer which will be dedicated to organizing branch accounts.

In time, a Barclays spokesman said, the bank could envisage equipping all its local branches with a computer. These could be linked to form a network, making the branch of the future a super-efficient business centre capable of processing transactions in seconds.

White South Africans Form Anti-Apartheid Party

Not all white South Africans are racist bigots determined to keep their country's black, Cape Coloured and mixed race population in a state of underprivileged near-slavery, the world was happy to learn today. Appalled at the increasingly savage treatment handed out to the majority of South Africans in the name of apartheid, a group of white liberal Members of Parliament announced that they had resigned their previous party's whips and formed a new anti-apartheid group.

To be called The Progressive Party, it would prove a constant thorn in the side of successive South African governments, and provide a legal and highly-public platform for the views of non-racists in the years of struggle which still lay ahead.

HERE COME THE GIRLS - CONNIE AND SHIRLEY MAKE THEIR MARK

With the world's pop music scene dominated almost entirely by male rock 'n' roll singers and groups for the past four years, the emergence of Connie Francis and Shirley Bassey to well-deserved stardom this year was good news for those who'd missed the sweeter sound of a female voice in the charts.

True, a 13 year old Brenda Lee had enjoyed an initial brief run of success in 1957 with *One Step At A Time* and *Dynamite,* but it wouldn't be until next year that she'd start the almost unbroken string of huge international hits which would qualify her for superstar status. And while there were many successful young black female artists in the US, few had yet made an impact on the national charts, let alone enjoyed international hits.

Connie Francis began her rise in 1958, when she scored with a re-working of the oldie *Who's Sorry Now,* sold a million and triggered what would in fact be a nine-year run of international hits. She'd consolidated that start with *I'm Sorry If I Made You Cry,* the Neil Sedaka rocker *Stupid Cupid* and *Fallin'* before entering 1959 with the flourish of *You Always Hurt The One You Love, My Happiness, Lipstick On Your Collar* and *Among My Souvenirs.*

A native of Belleville, New Jersey, and baptized Constance Franconero, Connie began playing the accordion at the age of four, made her first professional appearance at eleven, and took the advice of American star-spotter Arthur Godfrey that she drop both the accordion and her real name when she won his influential Talent Scout television contest.

No name-change was needed for Shirley Bassey, the Cardiff born daughter of a West Indian merchant seaman. She'd had an early shot at stardom in 1957 when her cover version of Harry Belafonte's *Banana Boat Song* charted briefly, but it was the out-of-nowhere smash she scored with *Kiss Me Honey Honey Kiss Me* in January this year which would enable the 20 year old with the huge voice to start building a stupendous international career destined to last for more than 30 years.

Consolidating her achievement, Shirley followed with a second British Top 10 hit (*As I Love You*), and while she would never compete with the likes of Connie Francis in the number of hits she'd score through the years, the ones she would have would be huge, and they would serve to reinforce the immense popularity she would enjoy as one of Britain's most successful concert, cabaret and TV performers.

RUSS FINDS HALF A FINGER NO BIG HANDICAP

Most people who lost half a finger in a machine shop accident could probably function pretty well without it after a while. But if you're a pianist, and you're determined to make it in showbiz, that absent digit end could spell ruination.

Russ Conway, the British piano player who spent most of 1959 with a single in the Top 20, certainly didn't seem to miss the end of the finger he mislaid in a factory. Following very much in the rolling pub singalong style established by Winifred Attwell a few years earlier, Conway just played so many notes so quickly, no-one could tell if he ever needed that joint at all!

For the record, Conway's hits this year were *Side Saddle,*

Roulette, China Tea and the Christmas-flavoured *Snow Coach*. Jolly, undemanding and generally interchangeable, they would prove to be the peak of Russ Conway's brief but rewarding brush with fame.

BARBER'S LITTLE FLOWER BLOSSOMS TO MILLION-SELLING SMASH

One-hit wonders don't come any bigger than the one The Chris Barber Jazz Band (former home of skiffle king Lonnie Donegan) had this year with *Petite Fleur,* a pretty little tune written by New Orleans clarinettist Sidney Bechet which featured the mellow tones of Barber's clarinet player, Monty Sunshine.

A surprise instant hit when first released in Britain during February, the single came to the attention of Bob Schwartz, president of the American Laurie Records label. Hearing what thousands of British record-buyers loved, he secured the US rights and had the satisfaction of seeing his gamble race into the US Top 10 and sell more than a million copies in the process.

For Barber, one of Britain's most popular jazz club performers throughout the 1950s and 1960s, and an early promoter of American blues artists who'd inspire the British R&B boom of the mid-Sixties, Bechet's *'Little Flower'* would prove his only taste of life in pop's fast lane.

Connie Francis - Bringing back the sweet sound of the female voice to the charts

SEPTEMBER 16

De Gaulle Offers Algerians Referendum

SEEKING A WAY OUT of the bloody civil war which continued to ravage the French colony of Algeria, President Charles de Gaulle tonight made a dramatic offer of a referendum aimed at letting the north African country's citizens control their own future.

In a nationwide television broadcast, de Gaulle said that within four years of peace being restored, Algerians could vote for a constitution of their own. He defined 'peace' as a year-long period during which less than 200 people died from terrorist activities.

Three alternatives faced Algerians, de Gaulle explained. They could choose to secede from France and become completely independent. They could opt to integrate completely with France. Or they could - and he made it clear that this was his preferred option - decide on independence in close association with France.

While commentators were quick to praise the boldness of de Gaulle's plan, they rightly predicted that it was bound to provoke a strong negative reaction from many of the European settlers in Algeria, their French supporters, a large number of French army officers, and the Arab nationalists whose bid for independence - and the violent methods they used - created the Algerian problem in the first place.

SEPTEMBER 14

Soviets Score Moon Hit

The first man-made object to reach the moon, Russia's *Lunik 2* rocket helped score a major public relations coup for the USSR when it crashed into the lunar surface today, only hours before Nikita Khrushchev's *Iluyshin* jet made a much softer landing in New York to signal the start of his first American visit.

The rocket, which took 35 hours to travel the 250,000 or so miles between central Russia and the moon, sent a steady stream of valuable information back to Soviet scientists monitoring its progress - including data on radiation, magnetic fields and the various types of matter to be found in space. Space, it would appear, was not a vacuum at all. As a Soviet spokesman explained: 'We now know it contains gas, cosmic dust and some larger particles of matter.'

SEPTEMBER 8

Macmillan Sets British Election Date

Britain will, on October 8, be given the chance to decide which of its two political leaders - the incumbent Conservative Party's Prime Minister Harold Macmillan, or Labour's Hugh Gaitskell - will represent the country at the Big Four summit planned for next May.

That was the date set by Macmillan today for the general election he said would determine whether British interests were presented by an experienced, established team of international experts led by him, or a delegation of inexperienced members of a Labour Party still split on the subject of nuclear disarmament.

Hugh Gaitskell, on a visit to Moscow, flew back to London at once, telling newsmen: 'A Labour victory is vital for the world.'

SEPTEMBER 24

Rolls Royce Unveil Phantom V

With all the understated pride for which the company was world-renowned, Rolls Royce unveiled their newest 'baby' to champagne-quaffing journalists in London today. The *Phantom V* proved worthy of the Rolls Royce pedigree, the ultimate in luxury motoring and definitely not of the same planet which produced BMC's *Mini*, production of which was hit by strikes this month in Birmingham. The price tag was inevitably higher, too. At a time when you could buy a decent three-bedroomed semi-detached suburban house for around £3,000 ($9,000), the *Phantom V* would set you back a breathtaking £9,000!

ARRIVALS

Born this month:
5: Andre Phillips, US Olympic 400m hurdles champion (Olympic gold 1988)
14: Morten Harket, Norwegian pop singer, songwriter (A-Ha)
20: Alannah Currie, US pop musician, writer (Thompson Twins)
21: Corinne Drewery, UK pop musician (Swing Out Sister)
27: Beth Heiden, US speed skating champion, Women's World Road Race cyclist, and NCAA Cross-Country Ski Champion 1983

DEPARTURES

Died this month:
22: William Edmund, 1st Baron Ironside, British soldier
25: Helen Broderick, US film and stage actress (*Top Hat, Swing Time, No No Nanette*, etc)
27: Solomon West Ridgeway Dias Bandaranaike, Sinhalese Prime Minister of Ceylon 1956-59

SEPTEMBER 17

BBC TV Buys US Movies As Cinemas Close

The giant Rank Organisation - Britain's leading film production and distribution company - today confirmed what everyone pretty well knew for certain - television was knocking cinema attendance figures for six, and the movie industry was hurting.
In a week dominated by news that BBC TV had bought 20 American feature films for broadcast over the next six months, the Rank statement disclosed that between 1950 and 1956, cinema audiences had dropped from an initial 1.396 million a year to 1.101 million - and this year's figures were already down 14 per cent on those of 1958.
There was also bad news for those who still preferred to watch moving pictures amid the rustling of chocolate wrappers and the coughs of consumptive smokers - more cinemas were destined to close. With 91 Rank-owned cinemas already shut down since 1956 and another 57 nominated for closure, the company admitted that even more will probably have to dim their house lights forever.

Khrushchev Refused Disneyland Day Out

HAVING VISITED THE Hollywood studio set of the movie *Can-Can*, met Shirley Maclaine and hung out with its leggy chorus girls, Soviet leader Nikita Khrushchev had one more excursion he really wanted to take before he headed for Washington and talks with President Eisenhower about Berlin – his heart was set on seeing Disneyland.

Today, someone had the task of telling Khrushchev he wouldn't get to meet Mickey, Minnie or any of Walt Disney's larger than life characters in the world's biggest playpen. His security couldn't be guaranteed.

So he was in a pretty bad mood before he sat down at the Los Angeles banquet designed to give him the finest of farewells. That mood darkened when, in a break

with the supposedly cosy tone of the evening, LA Mayor Norris Poulson made a hostile speech in response to Khrushchev's recent UN outburst when he'd threatened western leaders, 'We will bury you!'

A furious Khrushchev threatened to take the next plane home but was persuaded to let it all pass. The next morning, Khrushchev had further reason to sulk when the mayor failed to turn up at the rail station to see him off. His mood was to lift when the train reached Santa Barbara and he caught sight of the huge crowd of cheering, clapping people waiting to shake his hand. After obliging as many as he could, Khrushchev told press-men, 'I have seen some real Americans at last, and it seems to me they are as good and kind as our Soviet people'.

Callas Denies Onassis Romance

Maria Callas (pictured with Aristotle Onassis), the Greek-born grande-dame of opera whose close friendship with shipping magnate and fellow-Greek Aristotle Onassis had long set gossiping tongues wagging, today confirmed that her marriage had ended. Speaking in Rome, the majestic diva admitted that she and her businessman husband were no longer ascloseasthis, blaming the pressures of her international work schedule for an inevitable separation.

The 37 year old soprano superstar, who was born Maria Anna Cecilia Sofia Kalogeropoulos, strenuously denied there was any liaison between her and the 53 year old Onassis, multi-millionaire head of a huge freight shipping line and owner of Olympic Airways.

Terse Talks And Cool Chinese Reception For Khrushchev

Fresh from his summit talks with President Eisenhower, Nikita Khrushchev arrived in China this month to meet Chairman Mao Tse-Tung and other national leaders (pictured). His welcome was decidedly formal, and cool to the point of frosty, and it's believed the two leaders' subsequent meetings were marked as much by division as comradely affection. The world's two leading communists had much to disagree with in each other's policies and conduct. While Mao had been one of the very few to support the Soviet crushing of the 1956 Hungarian uprising, he was known to blame Khrushchev's 'liberal' approach to Russia's European satellites as the cause of that revolt. That, and Khrushchev's attacks on the brutality of Soviet dictator Josef Stalin - one of Mao's heroes - had made them uneasy bedfellows. While he appreciated the sheer physical weight of manpower Mao had at his disposal in military terms - some of which was arraigned threateningly at the Chinese-Soviet border - Khrushchev was determined his particular brand of Communism was the one the rest of the world should recognize.

Election Victory Means Supermac's Never Had It So Good

HAROLD MACMILLAN'S Conservative Party swept back into power today with an increased majority, confirming that the British electorate agreed with the Tories' campaign slogan: 'You've never had it so good'.

Admitting that his election campaign had 'gone off rather well', the Prime Minister saw his House of Commons power base increased with a final tally of 365 Conservative victories, a drop to 258 in an internally-divided Labour representation, and a slump in Liberal Party fortunes to only six seats. Supermac's victory meant that the Tories had now won three general elections in succession.

Conceding defeat early in the vote-counting, Labour leader Hugh Gaitskell agreed with the PM's summary that the result suggested that 'The class war is now obsolete.'

The Liberals saw their share of the national vote drop to a mere six per cent, and while former Oxford Union President Jeremy Thorpe was elected to Parliament, the TV reporter Robin Day failed to make the transition from celebrity to successful candidate.

The election saw the arrival of two women who would prove formidable additions to their parties' fire-power - Conservative Margaret Thatcher won her fight for the north London constituency of Finchley, while Labour's ranks were swollen by the arrival of Judith Hart. In his first cabinet shuffle, on October 14, Macmillan would appoint future party leader Edward Heath to the heart of power after a period of back-room authority as the Conservatives' highly-effective Chief Whip.

British Money To Go Decimal?

The first shots in the war to drag Britain's archaic and complex money system into line with almost all the world were fired in London today with the publication of a Royal Mint report which suggested that it would be sensible for the currency to go decimal.

At present, British schoolchildren had to come to grips with a currency which had four farthings to the penny, 12 pennies to the shilling and 20 shillings to the pound, with all kinds of twiddly extras (like the half-crown, which was 30 pence, and the guinea, which was one pound and one shilling) to muddy the mental waters even further and make maths tests a sadist's delight in the setting.

Mitterand Escapes Assassination

François Mitterand, the former French minister tipped by many as a politician to watch, escaped death by inches tonight as his car was chased through the streets of Paris by right-wing gunmen.

The Senator, recognized as one of the most dynamic socialists in the French National Assembly, managed to jump from his Citroën in the Luxembourg Gardens and jump over park railings to the safety of shrubbery.

Frustrated by missing their intended quarry, the hitmen took it out on Mitterand's car, riddling it with bullets before racing away into the dark.

UK TOP 10 SINGLES

1: Mack The Knife
- Bobby Darin

2: Here Comes Summer
- Jerry Keller

3: ('Til) I Kissed You
- The Everly Brothers

4: Only Sixteen
- Craig Douglas

5: Living Doll
- Cliff Richard

6: The Three Bells
- The Browns

7: Sea Of Love
- Marty Wilde

8: Travellin' Light
- Cliff Richard

9: High Hopes
- Frank Sinatra

10: Broken Hearted Melody
- Sarah Vaughan

OCTOBER 14

Swashbuckling Flynn Rides Into Last Sunset

ERROL FLYNN, (pictured) the hell-raising matinée idol who attracted as many column inches for his off-screen antics as he did for the work which financed his notorious lifestyle, died today at his Hollywood home.

He was only 50 years old. Born in Tasmania, the son of a zoologist, Flynn began his acting career as a member of the Northampton Repertory Company in England, and made one movie in Britain before moving to Hollywood in 1935, where his stunning good looks and natural athleticism made him an ideal choice for the string of derring-do action adventures in which he made his name - *Captain Blood, The Charge Of The Light Brigade* and *The Adventures of Robin Hood* included - before the war.

He did his bit for the Allied war effort by starring in morale-boosting thrillers which had him overcoming insurmountable odds to beat the (mostly Japanese) enemy, most notably *Objective Burma*.

Flynn's career miraculously survived a number of paternity suits and one criminal charge (which he successfully defended) of seducing an under-age girl, and while his acting skills continued to be in demand, the quality of roles diminished as his drinking increased. Typically, his autobiography *My Wicked Wicked Ways,* a remarkably frank and often hilarious no-holds-barred account of his life and good times, became an international best-seller when published in 1995.

OCTOBER 26

Soviets Film Dark Side Of The Moon

The first-ever glimpses of the usually-unseen 'dark' side of the moon were received by Soviet scientists today when *Lunik 3,* the space craft they had put into a successful lunar orbit, beamed footage back to Soviet Space Control. It's a remarkable achievement which gave the Russians a further public relations boost over the US space programme, which had so far had to trail behind while the Soviets grabbed the glory. More than 70 per cent of the previously unknown lunar landscape, described as 'more monotonous' than the side visible from earth, was clearly visible in the footage. The Soviet coup enabled patriotic scientists to name one large feature *The Moscow Sea.*

OCTOBER 7

Leakey's 'Lucy' Is World's Oldest 'Human'

An exhibition destined to create fierce debate among scientists, Biblical purists and white supremacists in coming years, opened in London today with the first public showing of a female skull said to be the earliest-known evidence that Man did evolve from apes and human beings originated in Africa.

The skull - called 'Lucy' by Dr Louis Leakey, the British palaeontologist who discovered her during excavations in a remote part of Kenya - confirmed long-held scientific evolution theories which ran precisely counter to the Bible's account of the seven-day Creation, and enraged racists who held that the world's white population could not have sprung from African roots.

'Lucy', who could be proved to have walked erect, was mute witness to the opinion first voiced by Charles Darwin in Victorian times.

JANUARY 16
JOHN MCENROE - THE SUPERBRAT SUPERSTAR

History does not record if John McEnroe (pictured) entered the world today in Wiesbaden, West Germany, shouting and protesting. If he did, it wouldn't be out of character for one of the greatest tennis players of all time who may, tragically, be remembered more for his appalling record of racket and umpire abuse than his outstanding skills.

His birthplace dictated by his lawyer father's US Air Force service, McEnroe won his first Grand Slam event, the mixed doubles, at the French Open in 1977 while still a student at Stanford University. But it was his sensational Wimbledon début at the age of 18 which established his formidable reputation and box-office appeal.

Although he only got as far as the semi-finals on that occasion, he did so as the first-ever qualifier to get that far, and the youngest. His marathon battle with Björn Borg to emerge as the 1981 Wimbledon champion, and his defeat of the Swedish ace later that year to win the US Open, signalled the arrival of a true genius and winner who, by 1992, had accumulated earnings of $12,227,622 to make him the third most successful player in history.

Marriage in 1986 to actress Tatum O'Neal (from whom he is now separated) and the birth of two sons did nothing to moderate McEnroe's explosive bad behaviour. The only player ever to be ejected from a Grand Slam tournament - the Australian Open in 1990, when he swore at an official - McEnroe should be remembered for the fact that only Jimmy Connors and Ivan Lendl have exceeded his 77 Grand Slam singles victories, and Tom

Okker his 77 doubles championships, 57 of them with Peter Fleming as his partner.

OCTOBER 7
MARIO LANZA, TOP OF THE POPS TENOR

Long before The Three Tenors achieved pop cult status, Mario Lanza attracted the kind of fan adulation most pop singers would give their eye teeth for, and his death today at the age of 38 robbed the world of a tenor who juggled the twin careers of opera singer and pop star with some ease.

Born in Philadelphia, Pennsylvania, Lanza (born Alfred Cocozza) grew up singing and in 1942 was discovered by Serge Koussevitsky of the Boston Symphony Orchestra, who advised him to turn professional. Signed to a 10-year deal with RCA Records in 1945, in 1949 Lanza was snapped up by MGM to make the first of a number of films, the most successful of which were the bio-pic *The Great Caruso* and *The Student Prince*.

The hits began coming in 1950, when *Be My Love* hit No 1 in the US charts, to be followed by a mix of operatic and pop songs, including *Vesti La Giubba*, *The Loveliest Night Of The Year*, *Because You're Mine* and *Arrivederci Roma*.

Ironically, it was in Rome, his adopted home since 1957, that Lanza did say arrivederci. His body weakened by the operatic tenor's traditional battle with weight increase and loss, he died at the Guila Clinic after suffering a massive heart attack.

MARCH 3
FRANK LLOYD WRIGHT - THE PEOPLE'S ARCHITECT

It's no exaggeration to say that Frank Lloyd Wright, the architect and visionary who died today at the age of 90, transformed and revolutionized American house design. Remarkably, he did so while keeping faith with traditional homespun ideals and aesthetics to create a series of exciting new possibilities in the use of new materials like concrete and prefabricated wooden sections.

Wright stamped his signature on many of the homes he designed by incorporating distinctive low sweeping roofs, prominent porches and hearths and great bands of windows. On a smaller scale, his prefabricated low-cost 'Usonian' homes often included built-in furniture.

Of the great public buildings Wright was commissioned to create, it's perhaps the spiral-ramp extravagance of the Guggenheim Museum in New York - only finally completed in 1995 - which has become the best-known testament to his genius.

AUG 21
SIR JACOB EPSTEIN - THE 'RUDE NUDE' SCULPTOR

Controversy and heated debate were never far away when a new work by Sir Jacob Epstein was unveiled. The New York born sculptor, who took British citizenship in 1907 once he'd decided to settle in England, simply had the gift of raising eyebrows with his rugged, primitive and powerful statues, never shrinking from showing male subjects in often fulsome glory.

Born in 1880, Epstein studied in Paris where he became deeply interested in primitive and ancient sculpture, and he used those influences to make his mark in 1907-08 with the 18 figures he produced for the façade of the British Medical Association in London. Their nudity and distortion scandalized many, as did the tomb he designed for Oscar Wilde's grave in Paris. Many of his works were physically attacked with hammer or paint.

Controversial to the end, Epstein learned that his sculpture of Christ, entitled *Ecce Homo*, had been rejected by Selby Abbey, just before he died.

Lumumba Held As Belgians Fly Troops To Congo

A LARGE CONTINGENT OF Belgian troops were reported on their way to the Congo today following anti-white riots inspired by the arrest seven days ago of Patrice Lumumba, the 34 year old leader of the Mouvement National Congolais (MNC), a fast-growing nationalist party dedicated to winning independence from Belgium.

The Congo crisis - by far the most serious Belgium has ever had to face in its west African colony - was sparked by a barnstorming speech by Lumumba during a meeting in a Stanleyville café. That broke up with Lumumba followers fanning out through the city's streets to begin a looting spree, with Belgian and aid charity buildings the principal targets. Unrest spread, with thousands of war-painted Congolese joining the chaos.

As police began to reply with gunfire to the hail of stones and spears which greeted their every appearance, the death toll rose to 75 and Lumumba went into hiding. He was arrested on November 1, along with a white couple - said not to be Belgians - who were sheltering him from the manhunt.

A former postal clerk and brewery salesman, Lumumba helped form the MNC in 1958 after a spell in prison for embezzlement. A delegate to the All-African Peoples Conference in Ghana last December, he returned demanding immediate independence for the Congo.

NOVEMBER 17

A Duty-Free Wee Dram Afore Ye Go?

Moderate celebrations in Scotland today as British Customs and Excise officials announced that international travellers departing from Prestwick and Renfrew Airports are to be allowed to buy duty-free wine and spirits. It's believed the same facility will soon be made available to passengers using London Airport.

Bottles purchased in the departure lounges will be marked 'Not for consumption on voyage' and handed to passengers as they board aircraft. Duty free drinks and tobacco have been widely available at overseas airports for some years, but the service's introduction to Britain was held up while Customs devised stringent security safeguards to eliminate an illegal home trade.

NOVEMBER 11

British Box Office Records Tumble To Ben-Hur

Universally tipped to dominate the 1959 Oscars ceremony in Hollywood next March, the Charlton Heston epic *Ben-Hur* opened in Britain today - and immediately started to break box office records to make it the runaway hit of the year.

Directed by William Wyler, and based on Lew Wallace's semi-biblical novel, *Ben-Hur* would in fact go on to win an unprecedented 11 Oscars in a competition which included such classics as *Some Like It Hot* and *Room At The Top*.

Highlight of the epic was the breathtaking chariot race which pitched Heston and arch-baddie Stephen Boyd against each other. A brilliant sequence which helped win the Oscar for special effects, it was actually directed by Andrew Marton.

NOVEMBER 26

Castro Appoints Che Cuban Bank Chief

In one of the strangest decisions of his short rule as Cuban supremo, President Fidel Castro announced that he had appointed Major Ernesto 'Che' Guevara the new head of the Cuban National Bank. A medical doctor by training, the 31 year old Argentinian is not known to have any qualifications which would make him the natural choice for such a key role in the rebuilding of Cuba's shattered national economy.

The son of wealthy parents, Guevara became a committed socialist and revolutionary after touring South America and witnessing the worst excesses of various fascistic regimes. Meeting Castro in Mexico, he accompanied him to Cuba - an island he'd never previously visited - in December 1956, becoming a trusted and valuable aide during Castro's struggle to overthrow the regime of Fulgencio Batistá.

It is widely believed that Guevara will act as Castro's spokesman in forthcoming talks with Russian and Chinese leaders. While fund-raising and economic support will be high on the agenda of those talks, details will be hammered out by others more able to juggle budgets.

NOVEMBER 17

Police Chiefs Slam New M1 Motorway

Less than three weeks after it was officially opened by Transport Minister Ernest Marples, Britain's brand new M1 motorway came under attack today when five local police chiefs criticized its design and operation. The motorway, which ran an initial 20 miles from the north London suburb of Mill Hill to St Albans, had claimed its first victims on November 6 with the death of two truck drivers in a pile-up. Incredibly popular with sightseers, the motorway's first weekend of operation was marked by the sight of hundreds of picnickers filling the verges of approach roads, all of whom the police had to ask to move on. Today's criticism was largely aimed at the decision to construct the M1 with concrete sections, rather than asphalt. Noisy and often bumpy, the road was also only two lanes wide at points - another reason for it being thought hazardous.

Europe Torn As Two Trade Blocs Square Up

EUROPE WAS PITCHED INTO what would be a lengthy period of confrontation today as Britain, Austria, Denmark, Norway, Sweden, Portugal and Switzerland signed a deal to form a trading union to rival the six-nation Common Market founded in Rome two years ago by France, West Germany, Belgium, Italy, Holland and Luxembourg.

By signing The European Free Trade Agreement (EFTA) in Stockholm, the 'outer seven' planned to at least upstage the 'inner six' Common Market countries, though the real plan was to absorb them into EFTA with a mixture of diplomacy and market supremacy.

British officials were known to be pleased with EFTA's establishing set of rules, which enabled the UK to maintain existing Commonwealth ties and tariffs - something the Treaty of Rome hadn't. That, and the fact that the United States was known to view EFTA benevolently, made the new association an easy concept to sell to the British public.

EFTA's expansionist philosophy was best expressed by Swedish Trade Minister Gunnar Lange, who stressed that it was not a closed club and that applications for membership from the Soviet Union and Eastern Bloc countries would be welcomed.

Derick Heathcoat Amery, re-appointed British Chancellor of the Exchequer in Harold Macmillan's recent cabinet shuffle, indicated that one of EFTA's first moves in forthcoming talks would be to invite the Common Market six to disband and join EFTA.

That's something commentators predict is as much likely to happen as the Soviet Union is to apply for EFTA membership.

UN Bans French H-Bomb Tests

France's nuclear test programme received a severe set-back in the United Nations today when the General Assembly slapped a ban on future trials in the Sahara. Responding to calls from all member countries in the region, the UN said that France should find a new, more remote location for its H-bomb blasts. It's widely believed the French will switch its operations to the Pacific.

Peace Prize Awarded To British Quaker

Philip Noel-Baker, the veteran British MP and Quaker who helped draft the League of Nations covenant in 1919, was today named as the winner of the 1959 Nobel Peace Prize. He will be presented with his medal at the now-traditional annual ceremony in Oslo on December 10.

A minister in the post-war Labour government, Noel-Baker recently retained his constituency, Derby South, while many Labour colleagues were forced to seek alternative work.

For more than 40 years he has campaigned tirelessly for an international arms control treaty.

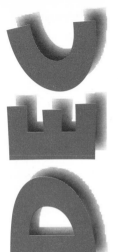

300 Killed As Storms Flood French Riviera

THREE HUNDRED PEOPLE were reported dead today when the French Riviera town of Frejus was hit by a 15-foot high wall of water, mud, boulders and debris which swept down a valley after a dam burst. As troops began the grim task of recovering the bodies of children buried in the sea of mud left behind, a shocked President de Gaulle ordered an official inquiry into the tragedy, declaring the region a national disaster zone.

Survivors of the carnage had few doubts on the matter. They said that local people had been predicting potential disaster for days, since it became clear that recent heavy rainstorms had created too much pressure on the nearby Malpasset dam. Cracks had been reported near its base, but they alleged that no attempt had been made to relieve the build-up.

Within minutes of the dam bursting, Frejus was devastated. A passenger train was overturned and overwhelmed, a power station washed away, telephone and power lines were torn down, and hundreds of cars and trucks were completely submerged, as were many houses.

One eye-witness said the flood ripped through Frejus for almost an hour, 'like a hammer'. Rescue teams who reached the area from naval helicopters reported as much as ten square miles under water, with houses and farms collapsed 'like piles of cards' and the railway line torn up 'like so much straw'.

Adam Faith - No 1 with *What Do You Want*

Chinese Communists Pardon The Last Emperor

Pu-Yi, the former - and last - Emperor of China, who reigned as a child from 1908 until he was forced to abdicate in 1912, was one of 33 'war criminals' pardoned today in Beijing by China's Supreme People's Court. Following a 10-year period of reforming hard labour, Pu-Yi was considered to have acknowledged his 'crimes', repented of them and shown determination to change his ways.

Subject of Bernardo Bertolluci's 1987 epic film *The Last Emperor*, Pu-Yi had been dragged from retirement by the Japanese in 1932, when they installed him as the puppet emperor of Manchuria, the Chinese region they'd invaded and occupied. Captured by the Russians in 1945, he'd testified as a prosecution witness in the Japanese war crimes trials in 1946 before being handed back to the Chinese communists.

Sentenced to house arrest in Fushun, near Mukden, Pu-Yi was described by foreign journalists allowed access to him, as 'an apathetic boiler-suited figure eager to confess his past crimes against the people'.

DECEMBER 1

Antarctica Made Nature Reserve

The vast frozen wastes of Antarctica became a no-go area for nuclear bomb tests and atomic waste storage today when the 12 countries which have territorial claims on the world's southernmost continent signed a treaty to create what is, in effect, the earth's biggest nature and science reserve.

Signatories to the treaty, including the US, the Soviet Union, France and Britain, also agreed to fix all existing territorial boundaries to avoid the chance of future disputes and outlawed the creation of military bases on Antarctica.

Additionally, the treaty - which can only be amended by unanimous agreement - granted free access to all parts of Antarctica to scientists of all nations. While it is vital that research continues into the region, the safeguards are designed to ensure minimal damage to Antarctica's unique environment.

UK TOP 10 SINGLES

1: What Do You Want
- Adam Faith
2: What Do You Want To Make Those Eyes At Me For
- Emile Ford & The Checkmates
3: Oh! Carol
- Neil Sedaka
4: Travellin' Light
- Cliff Richard
5: Seven Little Girls Sitting In The Back Seat
- The Avons
6: Red River Rock
- Johnny & The Hurricanes
7: Put Your Head On My Shoulder
- Paul Anka
8: Snow Coach
- Russ Conway
9: Rawhide
- Frankie Laine
10: More And More Party Pops
- Russ Conway

DECEMBER 14

Makarios Pleads For Peace As He Wins Cyprus Poll

ARCHBISHOP MAKARIOS (pictured) made a passionate plea tonight for the Greek and Turkish communities of Cyprus to work together 'in a spirit of great sincerity, with great respect for each other's natural rights'. He was speaking in Metaxas Square, Nicosia, to thousands of ecstatic supporters celebrating his election as the Mediterranean island's first President.

Some of those supporters chose to ignore the Archbishop's message of conciliation, staging a mock funeral for his Democratic Union opponent, who only attracted 33 per cent of the votes cast in the election – the first step towards full independence for Cyprus. Most were content to chant the Archbishop's name, dance, let off fireworks and drive around the capital sounding their horns triumphantly.

The Archbishop, spiritual and political leader of the Greek community, paid tribute to 'the heroes and martyrs' of the liberation movement, singling out Colonel George Grivas, leader of the EOKA guerrilla organization, for special praise and thanks. It was then he made his appeal for antagonism and fanaticism to cease. Seasoned Cyprus observers predict there is a long way to go before the mutual suspicion which divides Cyprus allows the transition to independence to take place amicably.

DECEMBER 14

Art World Mourns Stanley Spencer, Academy Reject

Sir Stanley Spencer, one of the world's most controversial and innovative painters, died today at his home in Cookham, the Thames-side village whose citizens he used as unwitting models for many of the large, often ribald canvasses many also condemned as sacrilegious. He was 68 years old.

Rejected as a potential exhibitor at London's Royal Academy in 1935 as 'too provocative', Spencer resigned as a Member and worked for many years completely outside the establishment. Religious paintings such as *The Resurrection in Cookham Churchyard* and *Christ Preaching At Cookham* depicted biblical events in a contemporary setting.

It was his stunning paintings and drawings of wartime shipbuilding on the Clyde which secured Spencer the commission to create a mural at Burghclere Royal Air Force Chapel. Drawing on harrowing memories of his WWI service as an ambulance man in Greece, Spencer produced a masterpiece which helped restore his reputation with the Royal Academy and earned him a knighthood in this year's New Year's Honours List.

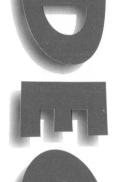

British Aircraft Giants To Merge

A new major player in the world's rapidly expanding aircraft industry was created today in London when two of Britain's biggest manufacturers - Hawker Siddeley and de Havilland - announced a merger to form a new company estimated to be worth £220 million ($660m).

In the biggest British link-up since the Austin and Morris motor companies merged in 1952, Hawker Siddeley - builders of almost everything from jet fighters to luxury limousines - offered £14 million ($42m) for de Havilland, manufacturers of *Vampire* and *Sea Vixen* military jets, *Comet* passenger airliners and *Blue Streak* guided missiles. Despite its formidable track record, de Havilland became vulnerable when its annual report showed a significant loss in 1958.

Modern Architects Hammered

Architects responsible for the design of new British suburbs, modern city centres and major projects such as nuclear power stations, came under heavy fire today with the publication in London of the Royal Fine Art Commission's annual report. The Commission, which included poet John Betjeman and sculptor Henry Moore in its ranks, called for a master plan for all future urban building to avoid what it described as the 'deplorably low standard' of much post-war inner city developments, and the 'drabness and mediocrity' of new suburbs.

Criticism was also levelled at the siting of 'ugly' nuclear power stations in areas of outstanding natural beauty.

YOUR 1959 HOROSCOPE

Unlike most Western horoscope systems which group astrological signs into month-long periods based on the influence of 12 constellations, the Chinese believe that those born in the same year of their calendar share common qualities, traits and weaknesses with one of 12 animals - Rat, Ox, Tiger, Rabbit, Dragon, Snake, Horse, Sheep, Monkey, Rooster, Dog or Pig.

They also allocate the general attributes of five natural elements - Earth, Fire, Metal, Water, Wood - and an overall positive or negative aspect to each sign to summarize its qualities.

If you were born between February 18, 1958 and February 7, 1959, you are a Dog. As this book is devoted to the events of 1959, let's take a look at the sign which governs those born between February 8 that year and January 27, 1960 - The Year of The Pig

THE PIG
FEBRUARY 8, 1959 - JANUARY 27, 1960
ELEMENT: EARTH ASPECT: (-)

Pigs, you won't be surprised to learn, have a taste for the good life. They possess a strong sense of luxury, can be extravagant and take great pleasure in pampering themselves and their loved ones. Pigs delight in the stimulation of the senses and enjoying *la joie de vivre*.

Despite this carefree and sensual attitude, Pigs can - when they need to - get stuck into work. Where they're concerned, it's all or nothing. But to compensate for their efforts, they reward themselves with little luxuries, holidays, trips or simply indulging in their favourite leisure pursuits.

This doesn't mean Pigs are frivolous and impractical. On the contrary, they are the most logical and down-to-earth people who may, at times, be considered cool and reserved. Blessed as they are with a paradoxical abundance of composure and self-control, Pigs simply don't allow emotions to cloud the issue.

Pigs love company and a social life, adore having fun and - with their light-hearted and sometimes sarcastic attitude - make amusing company. They find it easy to make friends as people are attracted to their vivacity. They are unpretentious and down-to-earth, and while they can be tactless, this comes from Pigs' essentially honest approach to life. Which means that Pigs are invaluable to have around in peace-making situations.

Some Pigs lack self-reflection and insight, but make up for that with big-hearted generosity which others take advantage of all too often. Though generally tolerant, Pigs can turn vicious when trapped or angered. If they feel their friendship and good nature have been abused, Pigs will dismiss any excuse and simply cut that friendship short.

Pigs put a lot of time and effort into their home life and excel in the culinary arts. When it comes to entertaining, Pigs can be excessive, extravagant and indulgent because they love parties, food, friends and having a good time. They also adore dressing up, and could be accused of showing off.

Pigs are basically honest, decent, generous, supportive and trustworthy people who are great to have on your side.

FAMOUS PIGS

Woody Allen
director, writer, actor
HRH The Duchess of York
Julie Andrews
actress, singer
Henry Kissinger
diplomat, Nobel Peace Prize winner
Elton John
singer, songwriter, flamboyant entertainer

John McEnroe
temperamental tennis genius
Ronald Reagan
actor-turned-US President
Tracey Ullman
comic actress, singer
HRH The Duke of Kent
Ben Elton
comedian, scriptwriter, novelist